Loom Knitting and Detail Instruction
Easy Loom Knitting Projects Everyone can Make

Copyright © 2020

DEDICATION

Contents

Loom Knit a Cap

MATERIALS:

Large round loom (I use a Boye set)

Loom hook (comes with the set)

Bulky yarn (again, I like Hometown USA <— around $3 each at Walmart, much cheaper)

You can make an adult size hat using one skein of Hometown USA. This includes a pompom if you're so inclined.

DIRECTIONS

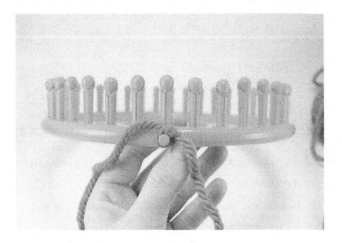

1. To start, tie an overhand knot onto the peg on the side of your loom. It doesn't need to be crazy tight. This is just to keep our yarn from getting away from us as we start the looming process.

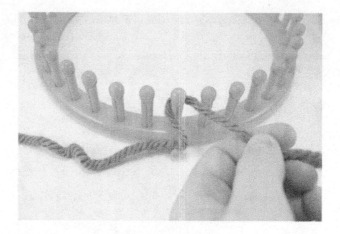

2. You're going to take the working yarn (the long bit as it comes out of your skein) to the right of the loom and wrap it around every peg in a clockwise fashion. Be sure to start with the peg just about your side peg. This will help with a visual cue to remember which peg is the first one.

3. *sidenote: If left-handed you can work to the left and wrap in a counter-clockwise fashion.

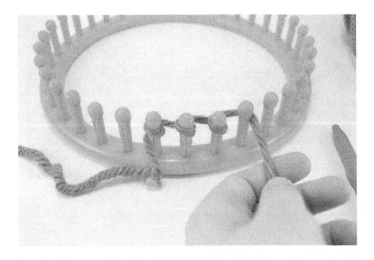

4. As you loop your yarn around each peg it is very, very important to keep the yarn nice and loose. Too tight and working the yarn later is a nightmare. Just keep it nice and loose as you go.

5. FYI – this is the E-wrap method, because you wrap the yarn around each peg in a lower-case "e" shape as it goes around each peg clock-wise.

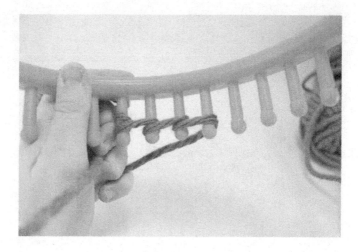

6. Now in case you're one of those crafters where the more details you have about the process the better, this tip is for you :) This is the inside of my loom. This is how the yarn should look from the inside if it is properly wrapped.

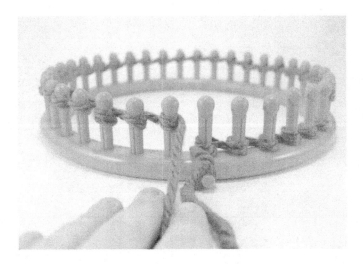

7. Wrap all of the way to the last peg.

8. Holding on to your yarn so that it doesn't get away from you, push the yarn down to the bottom of each peg, all of the way around.

9. Did you know how easy it is to loom knit a hat? It looks properly knit, too! I'm making a ton as gifts!

10. Wrap your yarn, loosely and counter-clockwise again around all of the pegs. Hang onto that yarn because the moment you let go that yarn will unwind off of those pegs like the dickens!

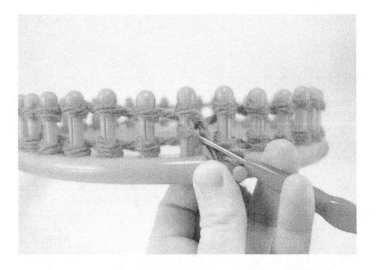

11. Using your loom hook grab the bottom loop on the LAST peg you wrapped.

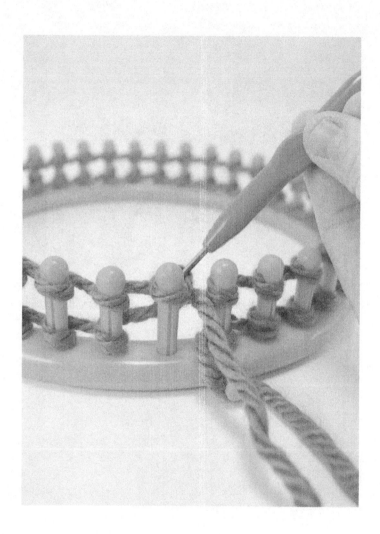

12. Pull that loop up and over the peg.

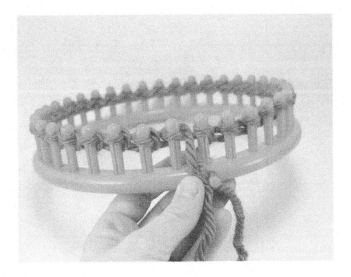

13. Continue pulling the bottom loops over the pegs all of the way around.

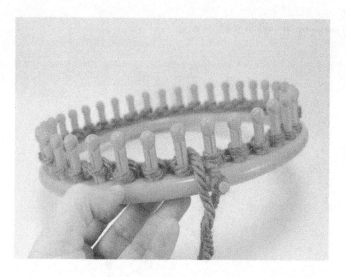

14. Push your yarn to the bottom of each peg, all of the way around.

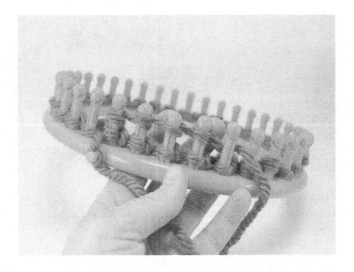

15. Continue the knitting process. *Wrap the yarn clockwise, loosely around each peg. Starting with the last peg wrapped pull the bottom loop up and off of the peg. Continue around the loom. Push the yarn to the bottom of each peg. Repeat from *.

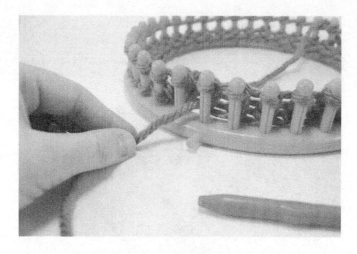

16. Once you get a few rows of knitting done you'll need to untie the tail from the side peg. If you leave the tail it messes with the tension and your rows get all strange.

17. Knit around and around until you reach a length of 10 inches for a tighter fit knit hat. Add more length for a knit slouch beanie.

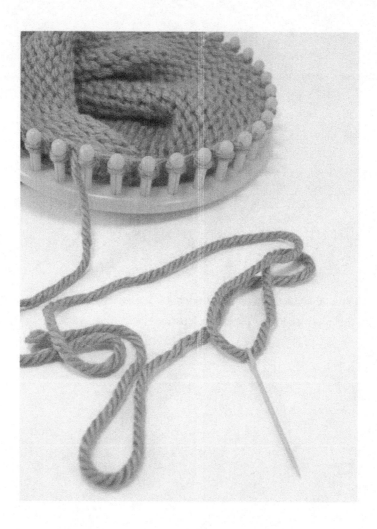

18. Cut your working yarn to 24-32 inches long and thread through a yarn needle (comes with your kit).

19. Push your need up through every loop on every peg, starting with the first (just above the side peg) and all the way around.

20. Once you've connected all of the loops on all of the pegs you can begin removing them with your loom hook.

21. This is the knit piece as it looks straight off of the loom.

22. Pull the tail of the yarn tight to pucker the piece and form the top of the cap. Take care to pleat and tuck as you tighten to make sure the top looks neat.

23. Make several stitches to keep the tightened area together. Finish by running your needle and yarn inside of the cap.

24. Weave in the ends and trim the excess yarn away.

Infinity Loom Knit Scarf

Knitting loom with at least 24 pins

Loom Hook

Yarn Needle

Gilmore Girls

MATERIALS:

Yarn

– 2 skeins Red Heart Super Saver OR

– 1 skein Lion Brand Homespun Yarn

– 1-2 skeins any kind of chunky yarn

Crochet Hook (optional)

Paper Straws

DIRECTIONS

1.   First things first. Start your yarn. Let me let you in on a little secret… pull from the

middle. Find the end of the yarn in there and pull out. This is going to keep your yarn from pulling away from you (which sucks)

2. To create a "yarn pen", cut a paper straw in half and carefully thread your yarn down the tube. I used a shishkabob stick to get it all the way down. This will help you to have nice even stitches across the scarf and save your fingers from too much twisty turning.

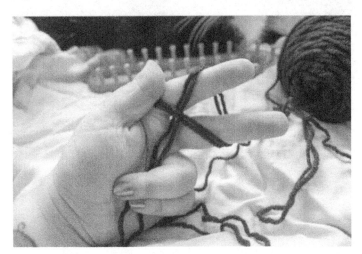

3. With the yarn pen pushed down toward the yarn balls, start with a slip knot with about 4-5 inches of tail. Secure the slip knot to the very end prong of the loom. Got it? Good.

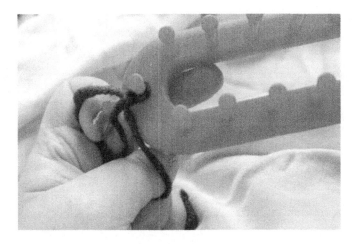

4. Now, depending on the size you want your scarf, I'd suggest using 12 on each side, so 24 total. Whatever you are most comfortable with.

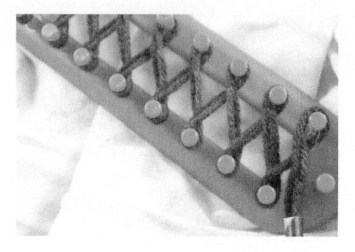

5. Grab the non-tail end of the yarn and put it between prongs 1 and 3. Wrap it clockwise around prong 1 and take it up in between prongs 2 and 4.

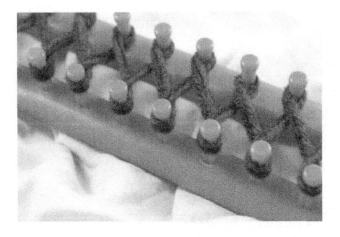

6. Wrap the yarn counter clockwise around prong 2 and bring it down in between prongs 2 and 4. Repeat the figure 8 pattern until you get to the desired width of the scarf. I had a 24 prong loom so I did the whole length of the loom.

7. Once you get to the last prong, weave your yarn (and yarn pen) back up though the last prongs you used on the opposite side. Repeat the figure 8 pattern back the way you came. When you get to the end, pull the yarn between two pegs on the other side and hold it with your finger.

8. Once you're double wrapped grab the loom hook. It's time to get to the fun part of your loom knit scarf.

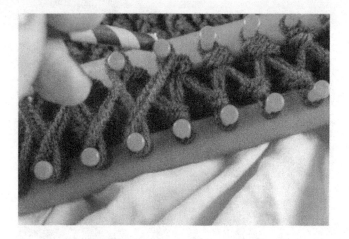

9. Knit up a warm and fun infinity loom knit scarf in just a few hours! A great project for beginners to create stunning hand made gifts in half the time!Knit up a warm and fun infinity loom knit scarf in just a few hours! A great project for beginners to create stunning hand made gifts in half the time!Knit up a warm and fun infinity loom knit scarf in just a few hours! A great project for beginners to create stunning hand made gifts in half the time!

10. Continue this process all the way around except for the last loop since it will only have one loop on it.

11. Once you've got it all done, the loops on the prongs down so they're on the bottom or the pegs.

12. Repeat the wrapping/hooking process for a lot of rows. Like a lot of them. Don't forget you're always going to end up with a single loop on then end. Don't worry about it. Seriously, it's part of the pattern.

13. After about 4 rows, remove the slip knot. Don't pull or anything, just simply take it off the prong.

14. As you get more comfortable with wrapping and looping you'll get super fast and you can get a scarf done in just an hour or two. Perfect for those with only a few hours a night and a lot of projects to do.

15. So yeah, keep going until your scarf is the desired length (about 5-6 feet). Then it's time to cast off. It's ridiculously easy if you use a crochet needle. I'm just going to send you to this video link because these guys explain it better than I ever could.

16. Once you've casted off, grab your yarn needle and attach the ends of the loom knit scarf with a flat seam.

Loom Knit Headband

MATERIALS:

1 Skein of All Things You Super Bulky Yarn (I used Pewter)

Darice Easy Knitting Loom Kit (Orange Loom)

Scissors

Tapestry Needle

DIRECTIONS

1. Wrap the yarn around the peg that is on the outer edge of the loom ring just once to secure. (You may also simply make a slip knot and attach it to your first peg on the loom if you prefer instead).

2. Holding the loom in front of you, pull the yarn to the inside of the loom. Wrap the yarn loosely around each peg clockwise, working around the loom counter clockwise, all the way around the loom. Be sure to wrap yarn around each peg.

3. Push the yarn down each peg so it sits toward the base of the loom.

4. Wrap the yarn around each peg again in the same manner as above. You will now have two rows of yarn on the loom.

5. With two rows of yarn on each peg, you will now take your loom pick and lift the bottom row of yarn over the top row on each peg working clockwise. Start with the peg that you just finished wrapping at the end of the round. This will hold your yarn in place as you work around the loom. Lift the first row over the second row on each peg and you will have completed your first row of knitting.

6. Repeat the process by wrapping your yarn around each peg, just as you did in step 2. You will then repeat steps 3 – 5, lifting the first row of yarn over the second row of yarn on each peg.

Continue this process until your piece measures approximately 6" inches in length.

Once your piece is approximately 6" inches in length, you will be doubling over the fabric. Find the first round that you knit and place those knit stitches onto the loom. You now have two rows of stitches on each peg.

Now, with a long length of yarn which is still attached to your loom and knitting, attach the end of the yarn to your tapestry needle.

Take the tapestry needle, and thread through each stitch on each peg of the loom. As you work around the loom, take the stitch off the loom once it's stitched to your length of yarn. Keep it nice and loose so it is not too tight on your head. Tie off and weave in ends.

Center Tied Section:

With a length of yarn and your tapestry needle, make two long straight stitches across the middle of the headband, working through both layers of fabric. Then, pull the ends of the yarn tightly to "cinch" the center of the headband. With a length of yarn, wrap it several time around the cinched portion of the headband. Tie off and weave in the ends.

Enjoy your cozy new loom knit headband!

Loom Knit Throw Pillow

GETTING STARTED:

Download the PDF for a set of portable project instructions. Read through all of the instructions before beginning.

ABBREVIATIONS:

cm—centimeter(s); g—gram(s); ew—e-wrap knit; oz—ounce(s); st(s)— stitch(es)

SIZE:

17" (43 cm) x 17" (43 cm)

MATERIALS:

#6 bulky weight yarn: Red Heart Boutique Twilight, 61% Acrylic/25% Nylon/9% Polyester/5% Metallic, 3.5 oz (100g), 59 yd (54 m) 2 skeins, color #9959 Mercury

Boye® 30-peg Bulky Yarn Loom

Loom tool

Yarn needle

16" (40.5 cm) square pillow form

SPECIAL STITCHES:

Flat Panel Bind Off:

E-wrap and knit the first two stitches.

Step 2: Remove the loop from peg 2 and place it on peg 1. Knit off peg 1.

Step 3: Move the remaining loop on peg 1 back to peg 2. – One peg bound off.

Step 4: E-wrap and knit peg 3. Remove the loop from peg 3 and place it on peg 2. Knit off peg 2.

Step 5: Move the remaining loop from peg 2 back to peg 3—two stitches are bound off. Continue binding off each peg in the same manner until you only have one loop remaining on the loom. E-wrap this peg and knit off. Cut yarn leaving a 24" (61 cm) tail and pull through last loop to secure.

NOTES:

This pillow is knit flat on the round loom

DIRECTIONS

1. E-wrap cast-on 29 pegs (one peg not used). Do NOT join for knitting in the round.
2. E-wrap and knit next row.
3. Continue to e-wrap and knit for 80 rows or until piece is 31" (79 cm) long.
4. Bind off using Flat Panel Bind Off (see Special Stitches above) leaving a long tail for sewing.

FINISHING

Fold piece in half with right sides together; thread tail onto yarn needle to side; repeat for second side; weave in ends.

Turn pillow right side out; insert pillow form; cut 24" (61 cm) piece of yarn and thread onto yarn needle; sew last side closed; weave in tail.

Loom Knit a Coffee Sleeve

MATERIALS:

Knitting Loom Kit

Charcoal Gray Yarn

White Yarn

Fabric Glue

Scissors

DIRECTIONS

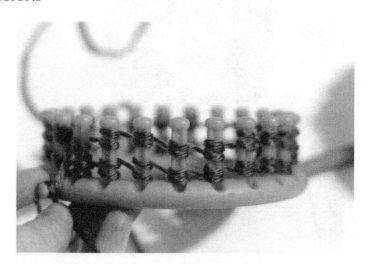

1. Start with the instructions that come with your knitting loom kit. You are going to be using those to knit a long sleeve with the gray yarn and the blue loom. The only difference is that you will be wrapping each peg twice then pulling those over two more wraps. TIP: Wrap LOOSELY or this project will not turn out correctly. Follow the instructions with the loom exactly except for the wrapping of the loom twice. Stop with the kit instructions before finishing off your project. The instructions are for how to loom knit a hat and obviously we are not making a hat!

2. Use the instructions to knit a tube about 6 inches long using this method. Now we are going to deviate from the how to loom knit manufacture's instructions to turn this into the monogram coffee sleeve.

3. Pick up the bottom of your tube and put the loops onto the loom from the inside. This will basically double over the tube that you have created.

4. Pick up each bottom set of loops and put it over the top loop. You now have a coffee sleeve but we have to finish off the top. Start with the second peg to the right of the loom as shown below. Lift off the loop and put it on the peg directly to the left.

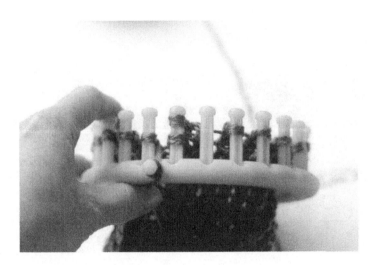

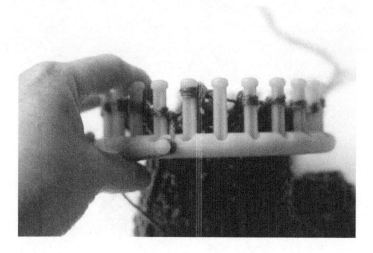

5. Lift the bottom over the top with your tool.

6. Then move that loop from the peg it is on to the peg directly to the right. Keep repeating all the way around the loom.

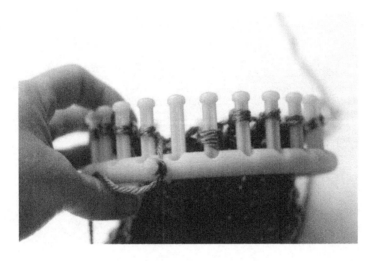

7. You will end on the last peg. Wrap the yarn end around twice and lift the bottom loop over the top.

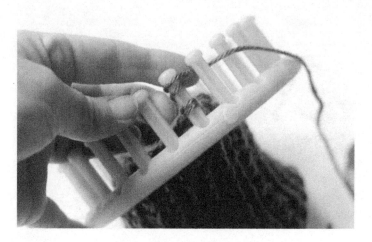

8. Repeat once more but with a single wrap.

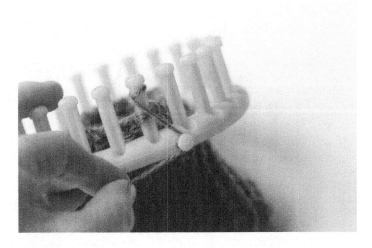

9. This time pull the end after you lift the bottom loops over the top.

10. You will be left with a sleeve and two ends. One from the beginning of your knitting and one from the end. Tie these two in a few knots and trim ends. Weave ends into the coffee sleeve.

11. Try the sleeve onto your mug for size. I found it worked best when the braided end I just finished was up.

12. Now you will need fabric glue and a contrasting yarn.

13. Just use the glue to draw a monogram.

14. Then apply yarn in the shape of the letter. I doubled up the yarn to create a fun monogram design on my coffee sleeve.

This fun beginner's how to loom knit project makes a perfect gift for Christmas. Make these in a variety of colors for everyone on your shopping list.

Loom Flower

MATERIALS:

A Flower Loom (I found mine at the craft store for just a few dollars)

A Loom Hook (the one shown came with the loom)

A Tapestry Needle

Scissors

Yarn (yarn shown is Red Heart Super Saver)

DIRECTIONS

1. To make a loom flower, locate the peg on the side of the loom, this is called the "anchor peg" reserve about 4 inches or so and tie the yarn onto the peg

2. Begin by wrapping the yarn around the peg directly across from the anchor peg as shown below,

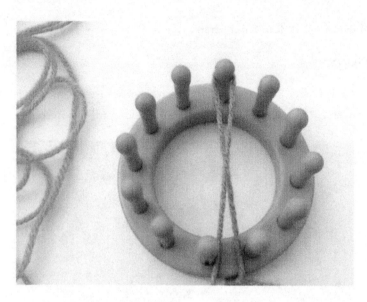

3. then continue in a clockwise fashion, always moving to the peg on the right,

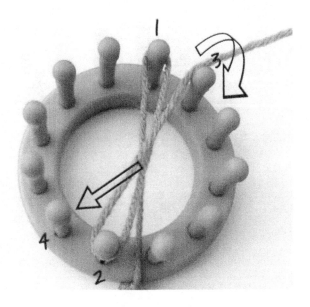

4. Continue all the way around as shown below:

5. We will make a total of three layers, so next you'll want to push this first layer down, using the hook tool if needed,

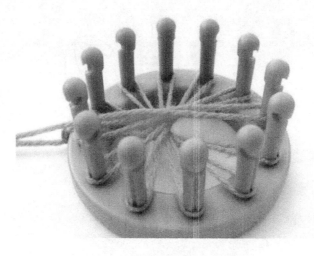

6. In the same manner, wrap the next layer, push it down, then wrap the third and final layer.

7. Push this layer down as well, then cut the yarn so that is equal to the other yarn tail.

8. Flip the loom over and bring both tails (you'll have to pull one of them of of the anchor peg) to the back and tie off. I made three knots in mine to get it nice and secure...

9. Select your flower's center color (same color or contrasting color) and thread the tapestry needle so that the ends are the same length.

10. Working from back to front, come up from the back in between two "petals" and go back in with the needle to the in between area directly across.

11. Do the same thing going the other way, this will make a "plus sign"

12. In the same manner, now make an "X" over top of the "plus"

13. Then continue until each in-between petal space has contrasting yarn in between it.

14. Flip the loom over once more and knot it securely. If you want to tie the flower to something, leave the tails intact, otherwise you can trim the tails.

15. Depending on your loom, you can either take the pegs off to remove your flower, or use the hook tool to lift each petal up and over the pegs.

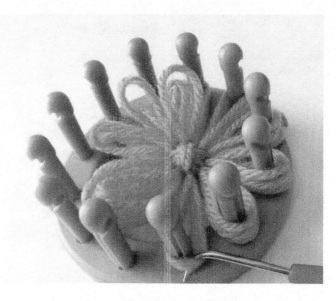

16. Do this all the way around...

17. And the flower is complete...

Loom Knit Leg Warmers

A 10 inch long loom is used in this pattern. For the Knifty Knitter loom set, this is the pink long loom. The 10 inch long loom from another set may be substituted.

The e wrap is used to knit back and forth to create a flat panel of knit. Change the color of the yarn after every 4 rows to create striped leg warmers. After the panel is removed from the loom, it is sewn together.

For a teen, you can use the pink long loom, wrap all 26 pegs and knit in a circular pattern to create tube knit, rather than flat panel knit. This is a variation of a pattern originally published by Provo Craft. The red round loom can also be used to knit these leg warmers. (I prefer the red round loom because you don't get the gap in the knit when knitting around around the ends of the long looms.)

DIRECTIONS

1. Holding 2 strands yarn as if they are one, cast on by e wrapping the loom one time.

2. E wrap the loom a second time.

3. Knit 4 rows.

4. Change the color to 2 strands of red yarn and knit 4 more rows.

5. Change the color to grey and repeat alternating 4 rows of each color until you've knitted 7 red stripes and 8 grey stripes, you will have grey on the loom. Continue on with the 4 more grey rows, for a total of 8 rows to make the grey band.

8. Cast off the loom, by sewing through each loop. (Don't use a crochet cast on or off. It makes the ends to tight to stretch when the leg warmers are put on.)

9. Cut the working yarn to about 24 inches. Turn the grey band under (toward the side of the knit you don't want showing outward). Whip stitch it down to form a cuff.

10. Also with the side of the knit you don't want showing facing outward, sew a seam up the side of the knit.

11. Cut the working yarn and tie a square knot.

12. Turn the leg warmer right side out so the seams are no longer showing.

13. Repeat the steps above for the second leg warmer.

**Note: To make these for a toddler, use 14 pegs and knit a total of rows.

Alice Wrist Warmers

MATERIALS:

Knifty Knitter blue small round loom (24 pegs)

Approximately 100 yards bulky yarn

DIRECTIONS

1. Cast on using the e-wrap cast on method.

2. Eight rows of K1P1 Loom Instructions: knit purl.

3. Knit all stitches for 20 rows.

4. For the thumb hole you will knit back and forth. Start by going in the backwards direction (counter-clockwise, if you loom knit clockwise). First knit peg 24 and 23 together. Then knit pegs 22 through 3 individually. Next knit pegs 1 and 2 together.

5. Knit two more rows and add a stitch on to peg 1 at the end. Continue to knit one more row and add a stitch on to peg 24.

6. Start knitting in the round once again for 12 rows.

7. Bind off, make the second one, then wear and enjoy!

Loom Knit Flower Earrings

MATERIALS:

Slip knot

E-Wrap Cast-On

Flat Knit

Gathered Bind-Off

Yarn:

Marly Bird's Chic Sheep yarn from Red Heart (aff. link)

Loom & Supplies:

12 peg Boye Bloom Loom (3/4" XLG gauge Flower loom). Knifty Knitter 12 peg loom also works. (Alternatively a 5/8" 16 peg as well).

Yarn/Tapestry needle (aff. link)

Pair of earring blanks (aff. link)

Notes:

*This pattern is not written in shorthand as it is made for someone who is new and just learning terms. Be sure to click the video to watch if you prefer.

*Flowers are made in the round.

*Flowers are made separately and attached to earrings

*Working Yarn means the yarn coming from the small ball of yarn in your supplies.

*Work the stitch or "knit over" simply means to lift the bottom loop over the top

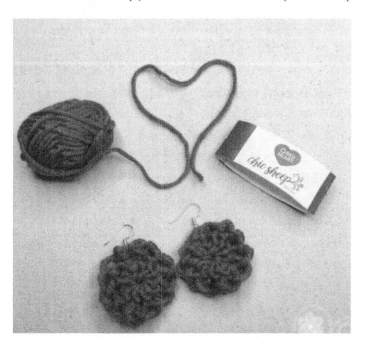

DIRECTIONS

1. To begin you need to put yarn loops onto the loom. This is called casting on. The abbreviation is CO.

2. To start, secure the yarn to the anchor peg with a Slipknot.

3. Place the slipknot on the anchor peg and tighten gently. Do not make it too tight because later you will release the slipknot after you have knitted a few rounds.

4. Next you will put a series of loops on the loom to begin knitting. The basic cast on method for loom knitting is called the E-wrap Cast On.

5. Move the working yarn to the inside of the loom between the first and last pegs.

6. Wrap the yarn around the first peg in a clockwise direction.

7. Repeat for the second peg and all the way around the loom. Make sure you don't wrap the yarn too tight because if you do, it will make it difficult to remove the loops as you work.

8. This technique is called E-wrap cast on because the wrapped pegs resemble a

9. NOTE: The pegs being wrapped in a clockwise motion with the loom being

10. worked in a counter-clockwise direction. In most cases it doesn't matter which direction you work or how you hold the loom. Work however it is most comfortable for you unless a pattern calls for a specific technique.

11. Push the loops near bottom of the pegs.

12. Wrap all pegs a second time starting with the first peg and ending with the last peg. Make sure you wrap in the same direction as you did the first time. You are now ready to begin knitting.

13. Beginning with the last peg wrapped, use your loom tool to lift the bottom loop over the top loop and knit off the loop. (There is a groove in each peg that helps to guide the hook.)

14. Continue around the loom by working peg 1, peg 2, etc. When all the pegs are worked you will again have only one loop on each peg. Each stitch is now "knit over".

15. Row 1: Wrap the working yarn around the loom above the pegs and hold the working yarn with the same hand that is holding the loom (or you can

16. temporarily secure it to the anchor peg); this keeps the yarn in place as you make a tighter knit. This stitch is called a "flat knit"; It is tighter and less stretchy then the e-wrap.

17. For this flower pattern wrap only 1 row and knit over, release the beginning slipknot from the anchor peg.

18. Flat knit only peg 1 once more.

19. Gathered Bind Off:

20. Wrap your working yarn around the loom 1 1/2 times and cut the

21. working yarn. Using your loom hook to guide the yarn through the loops as below.

22. Starting with peg 2, insert the hook below the loop and pull the yarn through; grabbing the working yarn from above the loop.

23. Repeat on the next peg. Repeat and work yarn through the loops on all pegs until all have yarn through them. Insert the hook into the loop on peg 2 again to make sure there is no gap.

24. Remove the loops from the pegs. Being careful not to twist the knitting into the circle, pull the yarn tail until the opening is completely closed. Using a yarn needle tie a knot near the center to keep it closed. Weave the tail to the edge of the flower to

the beginning tail. Tie tails in a knot.

Earrings:

1. Add 1 earring blank through one tail and tie tails in a secure knot. Weave tails back into flower center and tie in knot. Trim yarn tails, but not too short.

Make 2.

Knitted Nesting Baskets

SIZE:

Small (24 peg loom): 4" (10 cm) tall x 3" (7.5 cm) interior diameter

Medium (30 peg loom): 4.5" (11.5 cm) tall x 4" (10 cm) interior diameter

Large (36 peg loom): 5" (12.5 cm) tall x 5" (12.5 cm) interior diameter

MATERIALS:

#6 super bulky weight yarn: Red Heart Grande (78% Acrylic / 22% wool, 5.29 oz (150 g)>, 46 yd (42 m). One skein per basket; colors used: Small: Aran, Medium: Wintergreen, Large: Oatmeal

Boye® 24 peg loom

Boye® 30 peg loom

Boye® 36 peg loom

Loom tool

Yarn needle

Thread in coordinating colors

Sewing needle

See the Supply List for items you can purchase here.

GAUGE:

Gauge is not critical for this project if looms and yarn weight match the ones indicated above.

SPECIAL STITCHES:

FLAT PANEL BIND OFF

Step 1: E-wrap and knit the first two stitches.

Step 2: Remove the loop from peg 2 and place it on peg 1. Knit off peg 1.

Step 3: Move the remaining loop on peg 1 back to peg 2; One peg bound off.

Step 4: E-wrap and knit peg 3. Remove the loop from peg 3 and place it on peg 2. Knit off peg 2.

Step 5: Move the remaining loop from peg 2 back to peg 3; two stitches are bound off.

Continue binding off each peg in the same manner until you only have one loop remaining on the loom. E-wrap this peg and knit off. Cut yarn leaving an 8" (20 cm) tail and pull through last loop to secure.

I-CORD

Cast on desired number of pegs using e-wrap cast on. *Pass working yarn behind the cast on pegs and then back to the beginning. Hold the yarn in front of the pegs without wrapping (flat stitch) and knit off each peg. Tug tube gently every few rows to set stitches. Repeat from * until I-cord is desired length. To finish, cut yarn leaving an 8" (20 cm) tail. Thread tail onto yarn needle and insert needle through each stitch. Remove loops from loom and pull to gather. Sew securely then insert remaining tail into cord and trim.

DIRECTIONS

Note: Directions for smallest basket are given first followed by medium and large size in parentheses ( ).

SIDES OF BASKET

E-wrap cast on all pegs. Continue to e-wrap and knit until sides measure 5" (12.5 cm) / 5.5" (14 cm) / 6" (15.5 cm) when laid flat. Bind off using Flat Panel Bind Off. Cut yarn and weave in ends. Allow cast on edge to roll to form top edge of basket.

BOTTOM OF BASKET

Cast on 2 pegs. Following directions for I-cord, coil and sew the I-cord into a circle as you knit until it is slightly smaller than the base of the sides.

FINISHING:

Sew bottom to sides. Weave in all ends.

Made in the USA
Monee, IL
26 November 2024

71313302R00049